To Helen,

All best wishes,

Tony (A.A.M)

THE SURFACES OF LIGHT :
Fragments of the Mind

THE SURFACES OF LIGHT

Fragments of the Mind

Poems

A A MARCOFF

Hub Editions

Acknowledgements

Some of these poems have appeared previously in *Poetry Review*, *Blithe Spirit*, *Presence*, *Time Haiku*, *The Haiku Quarterly*, *Simply Haiku*, *Acumen*, *First Offense*, *Poetry Express*, *Weyfarers* and *Littoral*.

ISBN 978-1-903746-83-7

Hub Editions
Longholm
East Bank
Wingland
Sutton Bridge
Lincolnshire PE12 9YS

GAKE POEMS

... 'gake' poems after the Japanese word for 'cliff': they fall down the page like the cliff-faces of experience, with space all around, and they rise out as if from a sea into the sky of the mind ..

Professor J A W Bennett used to speak of 'the beetling cliff of experience' ...

dream

I
lay
down
by
the
river
&
became
the
salmon
of
my
own
pink
dreaming

sun

sundream
at
the
end
of
all
the
shadow:
a
golden
light
plays
on
the
fields
of
corn

river

here,
in
this
place –
the
river:
tears
of
joy
&
the
kingfisher
light
of
my
being

death

I
give
you
the
blossom
of
an orange tree
&
vanish
into
air
forever:
forever
is
a
light
summer
breeze

raindrops

in
a
sudden
breeze
raindrops
s
h
o
w
e
r
from
the
apple
tree

fall

the
green
rain
of
the
willow –
autumn's
f
a
l
l
i
n
g
light

love

the
pink
shadow
of
love
over
stone
flows
gently
like
water
into
your
morning
&
meaning

moon

a
radiant
stone -
it
gathers
into
its
own
light
&
rolls
slowly
through
slow
shadow

waves

the
waves
are
breaking
into
silence –
the
saffron
silence
of
a
saffron
sea

time

this
moment
passes
suddenly
into
light
&
memory
&
curves
like
stone
into
a
slow
stone
sea

butterfly

I
watch
a
white
butterfly
hover
over
the
road
&
for
a
moment
the
whole
world
seems
white

love

by
the arch
of
a
stone
bridge –
the blue light
of
a
damselfly:
&
at
the
water's
edge –
'*I*
love
you'

star

all
things
cohere
&
merge
into
the
white
star
burning
at
the
centre
of
the
mind

sun

mosaics
of
light
flicker
on
the
waters:
&
the
river
flows
on
into
the
sun

moon

out
of
the
passing
of
cloud –
the
white
revelation
of
moon
&
mystery
that
shines
through
all
dream

snails

after
the
rain –
the
slow
rhapsody
of
snails
&
the
silver
trails
of
their
silence

sun

I
stand
in
a
circle
of
light
&
the
sun
shines
its
golden
parabolas
of
silence

MINIMALIST BREATHS

in the silence of the hills
the sun
rises

in her sunglasses
I see Armageddon:
a polar bear
fishes
in white space

on the bus – rushing trees
& the pink uncertainties
of sunset

all my life
I have waited
for the moment
of death:
the stars are wild

I am
I am not
I am
as I walk in & out
of the mist

it is almost dusk:
seabirds
wheel over
the Thames
one last time

passing unmarked
another wave
on the shore

winter:
dark lanes
furrowing
the
mind

almost autumn:
the greyhound
merges with the mist

what is
the wisdom
of a slug?
the dark leaves
the damp ground

sometimes –
a sparrow:
sometimes –
just dust

I have
sudden thoughts of death
as the sunlight
warms my face
to the bone

the beautiful years
stepping
into a sunlit sea

dark is my memory,
& quiet – the quiet
of a ruin

the light
of the crocus:
the flourish
of
dream

dreams of darkness dreams of dawn this is it

a museum of moons shadows on the stone

swing my thoughts this yellow rock rose

bitter cold rim of moonlight a view of hills

one half of the waterfall becomes starlight

light strikes the mountains five peaks glow with snow

    Arabian light
    six horses speed
    towards the sun

    into the chasm –
    ten thousand butterflies:
    the colours of silence

    reciting
    the diamond sutra
    as the bath empties
    I dry
    my belly

Old Father Thames
in autumn sunlight
a golden Buddha

snow settles again
as it darkens – crows raucous
from the graveyard fence

sunlight glints
on the railway line:
wild geese
fly swiftly
overhead

the life of the river –
blue light
& a heron flying

buttercups
as the highlight
of the day

little girl
swinging in the rain –
her pink woollen hat

over
Cissbury Ring
fifty seabirds
turn the sky
white with wing

all around
white butterflies
catch the hill breeze

olive coloured leaves
two small blue flower stars
&
the rolling hills
of heaven   [after John Martin]

a *partita* by Bach:
the summer rain is radiant
with light

a cormorant
perched
in a breeze

dawn
as Revelation:
I walk
out of starlight
on to grass

immense light
on the line of the river:
a single swan
bends
her neck

a walk
in a cemetery:
I am alone
with
the grass & the sun

one
morning
in the autumn –
mist fell
cavernously

we are walking
hand in hand
into the colours
of memory:
you showed me a rainbow

I long for the lakes
& the mountains:
a stone
falls
into the pool of my mind

dawn again:
a white bridge
spans the years
& seabirds fly
through my memories

cold December morning
the yellow berries
wet with rainwater

the sound
of a violin –
light
shimmers
on the water

the transformation
of the ground
into
petals
of light

a stretch
of Old Man's Beard
along the hedge:
a hard sun,
shining

poised
on the threshold
of a moment –
a heron,
fishing

overgrown –
a cricket pitch:
the echo
of willow
& memory

out of
the darker possibilities –
a butterfly
broken
amongst blue graves

this & that
in a deep white landscape:
ah, when the snow is gone
I'll walk once more
on moonlight

the sound
of a woodpecker:
I look up
into the world
of the sky

in the playground
children slide into the sunshine
time after time

still more
cherry blossom haiku –
the mind
a white page

sunshine after cloud:
a gold tree bursts
into a gold silence

along the shore
a pregnant woman
is walking –
the waves in the depths
of her eyes

the waves
whiten on the shore
& return
into the deeper myth
of water, & silence

around
the statue
of Gandhi –
all the blossom
he could wish for

a white star
the old canal
I walk
into the darkness
of silence

standing
amongst the blossom –
I look out
at the floating world
of the sun

this is
the nature of a dream
that the scales of a fish
become
the rainbow of the sea

POEMS

flame

it is so,
codex,
the saffron ordered swerve
of the shore
in umbra,
the curve & image of a great bow,
       where
monks walk in a line –
all in a flow
& beautiful to the eye,
pilgrims
difficult
       as
the sea, & purposive

what is ignited,
& most lovely & aspired,
       is
the residue of language
broken
into ritual
(inward & still moving) –
       the mind
       a core
       of fire
scorching the wide sifted sand –
the bend & scar
of some pitched pathway,
the flower sublime
& the seed sown & burnt

          where
minds begin
to prospect,
& to summer

the monks
call us into experience
on the old sifting shore:
this is meditation,
the fire
that
fills
the world
with a scarlet emotion,
becomes
this curved
primeval temple,
this urged
latency & search
of
the sudden surging
flame

the wave

I find a way into the grove of my eye – & the present grows
dark with oils like an olive.

Mosaics or mascara fall with the twilight into the face of the
night, & there is a distinct & vital shadow-play on the wall
of experience. There is a transformation of the world, the
fragments of drama, & a darkening. My lips are rouge &
potent. I speak of God in the time it takes for the earth to
turn as the moon gives way to light in the halt & the image
of now, light shorn of dogma, & fractured. Time is a
changed spiral.

Columns of dust rise from the world like moments, lovely &
expressive.

I know the life of the moment.

I know the white star, & the wave & weave of words –
"When all is said & done".

Let me speak in the movement of the hour.
I *will* speak as if my tongue were the white of a star in a sky
becoming old.
How light is soft & fragrant!

As dawn begins to move with the dust into light that is local
& fascinating, I stand fast in an ancient empty amphitheatre
surrounded by the blue Aegean & whisper the word 'God'
ninety-nine times in the sun that is radiant with meaning.
The word remains – the word remains imbued in the stone
like some mysterious spell.

Last night the stars fell from the sky like wishes, gorgeous as
surprise & light & gleaming.

Now I stand in the olive grove of my vision & gather into my being the light of God, which is difficult to behold – " The people who walked in darkness have seen a great light".

Everything rolls into a wave, & thought, & rises – immense with time. This is the possibility of a world yearning for worlds. This is God calling for God to be heard in the core of experience, as the word expresses this great empirical presence in the light of the wave of the moment.

devotions

I turned
    towards
        the light
    atomic
    &
it was
     pure
     dawn
a pure
morning
    of pure
    summer
&
the sunlight
       poured
into me
like
  a waterfall
     a cascade
         of
          stars
&
in
  the outline
of
    the world
there were
figures
    moving
like
waves

&
the vision
  touched
    me
a secret power
my eyes
  were
deep & brimming suns
that
flowed
into
  the
  moment
with
  unaccountable
life
 &
presence

& the light was
   poised
   like

an unfamiliar dialogue
conducted
in
 blue

space

             a
watercolour
             universe
a
sketched
             astronomy
of
             shining
mind
shining
             like
deep
word

memories
     are
rainbows
that
     span
             the arias of time
(arches of
             iconic colour)
or prisms
             of
the presence
             of
the ruby
             of
God

I turn
into
the light atomic
& whisper
          of
      hollows
(white stars & wishes)
& the dark birds
          &
roses
of
unreflected
rock

the Air

the sun shines over the bulrushes -
        dazzling
        as mind:
I touch the book of light
&
the fable of the air:
the grass
        defines
        the spring –
a green ink & continent
of ancient tense & script:

the waves of the air
are inscriptions of the wind on the water
I see island within island
God within God
the concentration of all light
& the forms of the page
move me
        into
            that white
                flow
        of a stream
of light –
the rhythm
    of
      all things:

Eternity
is
    so relentless
& beauty's
        on the air:
I seek the world
of the eye:

it is real
as
ground
    &
stone & petal
or
sunbeams
that cohere & stream
through the matrix
        of
the Earth:

I write
the Alpha & aria
of the air:
I write the morning
of the star:
the Earth is raw with air
& things that move & flow
like birds of the sea –

                white
                with wing
      & singing
                of
      the sun:

      the world is moving
      in my blood
                like sunrise
      coursing through the godhead
                of
                the dawn –
      a deep red light & orb
      a chord rising
      into
      joy:

      at the end of forever & the empty page
                a petal
      falls to the ground –
                a crimson flame:
      & the Angel breathes
                air
      into the rocks of the mind –
      the lock
      of all Eternity:
      I walk
      into the wilderness
      like a cause –
      moment by moment

Composition

the cool & swerve of the shore,
more marvellous than dream:
Leviathan heads off into
blue space – vast symphony
of sea: we are walking
at dawn watching the sun
rise from water as light
penetrates every aspect of our world
with visibility: dawn
comes like a wave: this is
the sea of light & dream,
sea of salt & tongue & sun:
the waters are massive & unearthly,
as horizons curve into the distance
like blue myth: the white flight
of seabirds is hieratic,
a prophecy of light & sky:
waves come & go
like thoughts we surf
in the imagination of the spray:
inner light, a mind of sea ...

look, the sun is rising in this sky –
a revelation, & the waves of the sea move
with light: we are celebrants
of the waves & the white chorus of the birds:
we walk into morning poised
on shifting sands, with footprints
for a moment becoming sea
in time, in the cool & swerve
of the beautiful shore, this dream
everlasting ... imbued with the deep
blue dawn of God & bird

the Aria of the Sun

this golden knowledge,
atmosphere of light:
an orchestra white with time
creates an aria of sun:
the chant & drift of song
substantiates the air itself
as the music of joy, & touch:
it rings with dawn,
the coming of the bird,
sun lyrical with rays of light, & flower:
it is the Eden of our love – reaching
for that green nostalgia of the apple bough,
the core & key of all our vision:
light is the cascade,
the glancing on the surface
of the world, this moment now:
flowers grow into blaze – the daffodils
of thought, as we move on the stream
of sunlight into summer:

we are born into mystery –
this music of the rising sun,
green tree of golden apple,
the grove glowing in the morning
when the sun is too beautiful to look at:
but I see God, dreaming of a white dawn,
& all the flowers, the sunlight
sown & scattered in the fields:
listen, it is an aria of light & space,
the bloom & the way of the daffodil dawn,
when music is the consciousness of light:
illuminations: scrolls of sun: script,
or blossom of our thinking sung & scattered
on this stream of thought

the echoes of snow, & light

I sing of snow.
I sing of snow.
a crow flies over the snow –
white anchorage of memory –
aura & glow:
I walk into the beauty of stillness
that is curved & unbroken,
& my tracks become the fragile past –
steps that mark this landscape now:
a crow flies over the snow –
a shadow on the air above a vacancy of white,
a slow sea of snow that confronts this shadow:
& I hear everywhere the echoes,
echoes of memory,
echoes of snow,
the clash & glare of light on snow,
voices of winter
& the quiet sounds of paths that filter
through the winter
woodland:

I sing of snow,
drifting through the mind
with all the radiance of a winter sun,
pale, elemental snow,
slow descant of its song, or canto,
holy & wild & authentic:
& as I stand on this cold, still land,
I am alive to the core of my being –
pierced through with God,
in the central light of a psalm of old,
in the great white wheel of this horizon:
ah, these passing moments,
steeped in the reality of light here,

the all-pervading desert of the empty light
that settles on the snow
with the promise of more to fall,
the slow fleeting nothingness
of snow falling on snow, or
memory on
memory

The Dream of the Nun

(for Sister Eve)

It moves like lava, her dream,
Geologically, meditatively,
And instils in her mind
A sunlit glow.

She is there, alone,
In the fatal wood.
She is quiet & real,
Violet, white.

Time moves in her blood,
A silent stream.
It is as young & as old
As this moment.

She can see His eyes,
Imbued in the wood.
And her mind is arterial
With dreams.

She walks through the wood
With a crucial joy,
And the light itself
Is scarred.

Time now becomes His blood,
And moves over stone.
His body *is* the sacred wood,
And the trees are bone.

The Life of Wolves

Do you have a choice in the journey when, under a full moon, you tend wolf? As you go along the paths, which are faint by any standards, you have a savage tongue between your teeth, while the vegetation around you might be construed as a jagged savannah.

There are pools here and there along the way, and these are luminous, and full of stagnant water. And your wild and hungry eyes are set on your destination – somewhere you have thought about long, long ago, when you were hunting with that nebulous pack in the forests of your mind and your mysterious birth.

And this sudden, ruined terrain appears to you. It is born of the dawn. And as you walk through the wasted landscape, you *know* you have been here before, yes, you *know* it was from this very place that you started, years ago. And now again you hear a voice, with its strange chant or incantation, and *you see it there, that vision,* once again before you.

It is a vision of an egg, complete with the stones of your own consciousness, a snake, the hanged man, a wonderful field of human breasts growing from the ground, the mind, your own footsteps burning in snow, a spider, the mirror of an emperor, marble eagles stricken by lovingkindness, and a cathedral constructed from death and steel.

And the last thing you see is a molten ruby river, down which you are drifting in a small canoe. And in the sky above, shining down on everything, is the full moon, in the light of which you are searching once again for the wild and nebulous pack you hunted with in the ruined forest of your birth, long, long ago.

voices : a genesis

"she sang beyond the genius of the sea"
                                    - Wallace Stevens

ICON: she has not turned away before now ... she does so
& sighs again ... I thought to give
          her image in this room a kind of level pagination ...
but she would have some other
          satisfaction, so she says ... an audience in the
evening by the sea ... where then do
          we go from here?

AGON: what you want would be no more than virtual
anyway, so perhaps it's better to give
          way ... I feel you've been too hard with her though
it's not so much your mode of
          commerce as your local disadvantage to provide a
width of view ... it's not the sea she
          wants but visibility ... which is to say the shore, the
beach, the sand ... as once it was
          when things were mutually reliant not submerged ...

ICON: what happened to us then that we could be so silent
for so long .. so far removed ...
          tell me, what kind of cadence has the shore ... has it
a song?

AGON: its cadence is the most exact & patient you will
find ... give it time & it will calm the
          mind...

ICON: you see she smiles ...

DEON: why don't you take her by the hand & lead us all away from here ... take her to the
shore where we can see the sea, where she can sing without compulsion through the
evening ... be kind to her, for she is generous & in pain : you would not lose her ...

AGON: here then is the correct terrain, an ordinary beach : it could be May ... three of us are
on the beach with her, three old men ... how tired we must look & pale ...

DEON: the evening light becomes her rouged lips ...

AGON: the smooth horizon's geometry ...

ICON: silent as the distant bay ...

AGON: the metal motion of the waves, constant, yet becoming broken as it nears our
vantage ...

DEON: bringing weeds ...

AGON: a molten blue ...

ICON: a range of trees along the shore ...

AGON: a sheet of rocks ...

ICON: a tracery of leaves, the clouds – the colour ...

DEON: of lamb's blood ...

ICON: water shades of nightingale & grey that wash up weeds like wire ...

DEON: the cat's eye leaves ...

ICON: shimmering ...

DEON: from under the cold stones ...

AGON: can you hear the song?

DEON: I hear it now ...

ICON: its warm horns bring blood to my lips ...

AGON: the genitive of water ...

ICON: the trees that line the shore are like a dark green aria shaping arches in the sand ...

DEON: like beauty & the vegetable the weeds are chords ...

AGON: & it will last ...

ICON: at last we know ...

AGON: that the song is made of bone ...

DEON: that the child will be by morning ...

ICON: that she will be free ...

AGON: that she was of the sea ...

DEON: & we can say we knew the tension of her voice ...

AGON: falling like water ...

ICON: or like blue & certain shadowing ...

the river of dawn

out
of this interface
      of
      light & dark –
the light
deflected
      mind
to mind
to matter defined –
      a fact
or the entire raw diamond
      of
our thinking:

& dawn is
      rivered,
         universally –
among yellow fields
& silver mountains,
& moves
      into
      the current
of awareness,
the journeys of light,
& the wild,
& the possible,
& the white:

& we are
         alive
by joy
         to think
of thought –
the dawn
we call
God:

& *it is our great love*
         that is
our one great hope –
this broken bracket of mirror & rose –
the latent, coruscating light
         we live –
that egg of bone & fire & everlastingness:

& we move
into
         the river
         of
         sunrise,
as the nothingness
& all potential
give way
to watercolour shapes
of being:
a faint pink sky:
it is
dawn
in the depths
of
the mind

the sun & the grass: a landscape of impressions

Softly the breath in this light & beautiful world, dusky
voice that penetrates silences, words that emanate from
wonder & breath & moment ...

There is a scattering of snow & a silence greater than the
hills fills the land as far as eyes can see. Sparrows cluster
in a breeze, grass broken here & there, like memories. A
cormorant perches in the silence of the water, a millpond
where the sun catches the feathers of the birds in white
illumination & surprise. Leaves cover the railway
embankment & I can hear the sounds of morning
accumulate as seabirds rise as one from the waters & scatter
into the sky like a script, cawing, cawing, cawing with the
sound of the sea. They form hieroglyphics of a deepening
light, a tracery that gathers & then fades quite suddenly.
Further along the road, one single seabird wheels through
its own white curve.

This whole landscape seems declamatory & wild.

A deer runs, bounding, through open fields, running in
wonder & joy at its own lovely freedom. There is lightning
deep in my mind. A wilderness of light & space, this
winter, gathered into a hard sky, now bright, & cold. We
walk into that panorama of distant trees, the land sparse &
harsh as we go. Crows collect in fields. Light stirs & bends
into morning. Could these views summarise nature, the
level & beauty of land? Light ascends into the joy of my
thoughts. High above, those seabirds swirl through haze,
their wings catching what light there is. This glow, or
dispensation, of winter.

I can hear songbirds near the bulrushes & three seabirds circle once more overhead. In as much as we are walking, we are alive to the core, & understand something unspoken on this wild, mysterious way. The waters nearby are still as stone. So many small birds flit back & forth among the reeds, & the air seems thronged & exciting. This moment is a distillation of itself.

I remember how that tree looked in autumn – draped in fire, crimson.

The woods are quiet, ghostly now, with wisps of growth upon the ground. The river flows on into the sun, light frayed, glowing. What could be more invoking than this view of clouds drifting in brief shapes that ever change with winter winds? The sky is alive with bird & sun, the seed of the sun sown & piled up high with light, until slowly this hour begins to fade & day comes to an end, the servants of Death upon the hill, waiting like trees...

in no
particular hurry
wandering
along the road
in cold weather

the temple of worlds

the sense
of God
in a mystery of cloud

(chord)

an altar
& the thought of a star

(chord)

a blue helium
flower
& the mercury of mind

(chord)

the sun
        curves
into a wing & a way
&
light flows
over the bridges
        of
this nowhere

the sun
        is
our circular dream –
a golden density
        of
dream

witness
the hands
        of a nun
as she touches
        a
        small bird –
(the leaden silence of her lip)

seven columns
        of
        the temple
        dust
rise up
    & become
                seabirds
        &
the world
        slips
through
        the mind
                like
quicksilver

the sky
flows
    into
        a star

 a star
    that
       is
          burning
in the temple
of
worlds
as if the mind itself
      were
taking
shape
like a white hawk
speeding through thought

(chord)

ah,
  such
    a wild
       fire dance
         in
           the contours
of
this endless
     endless

    space

(chord)

blue & rose: a Picasso text

Born by the sea. Returned to the sea. Metamorphosis of
rock & wave. Canvas of sun & prophet of colour – the blue
of his enduring, unlimited eye. I can see a girl with a dove,
a harlequin, mirrors in the mind, his soul becoming with
every brushstroke the essence of this life. There is hunger &
fear too – his vision of the street, the poor, war. "Who is
responsible for these horrors?" "Why, you are, of course".

A contingency, an abstract of Cube, Africa, Totem &
Artery - & a Horse in the grip of Terror. The feral sun.

The women are much more than themselves. Jagged icons,
angular, lines of vivid starlight colour, redemption, the
tragic shadow of the world, an amazement: & still fall the
bombs. He is a magician of the brush on the level of
consciousness. A guitar, a sketch, a mother & child. A
clown drawing on clowns. Blue jazz. Blue theatre. The
outline is energy, everything reduced to the naked line, the
colour of the eye changing in the game, concentrated
picture & object. The wild sculpture of reality: war &
peace.

After dreams in blue & rose – the universal shock expressed
as mask & geometric grimace. And yet it is the Woman
who remains our icon, focal, enchanting: image of all time:
soul of the stars, & archetype:

> the model
> sits there
> draped in cloth:
> wonder, stillness,
> breath ... & blue

a Rothko text

Red rectangle. Red density. A temple rouge within,
within a temple rouge with infinity. The sense of the
sacred, shown, messiah. A red sail in a deep red sea. I
can see into the soul. It is not random, not yet broken. I
am in the presence of the mind darkly – in the presence of
some quiet vision of God absolute, the quiet of a hushed
volcano. The potency. Apollo & Dionysus break the
deadlock.

I am imbued with colour. Cataracts of colour. Flow, &
stillness, mingled together. My eye is at peace with this
ancient world, washed, pure, dense. I go into tranquillity.
Pigment of red. Pigment of black. A man who moves
into grey & black. He calls it not art but "communication
on an exalted level of experience".

How close to blood are the canvasses of that searing,
graphic brushwork, & imagery! The tautologies of
darkness, of colour, erupting. His last act in despair, the
sharpness on the wrists, his life flowing out & beyond. "I
curse God daily because men are born to die".

And so here I stand, offering to God these his paintings &
words & sacrifice & dance of fire & flame:-

> approaching the temple
> I bring
> thoughts of rouge –
> & last things:
> & last things

Orphée

The mirror is infected with the labyrinths of death. Hitherto she has come and gone by this mirror, through this mirror, beyond this mirror to the windswept corridors of a Hades in slow motion. She is the messenger of death and one day, with her motorcyclists as her wings, she will drive in the terminal chevrolet to collect him, the poet whose name is Orphée.

He has already seen her once, and her beauty has burned his mind. She has already seen him, from the mirror infected by death, and his beauty has transformed her heart.

And he sits at his desk in the house of his dreams, working. He types the word 'cataplexy', and for a moment he lives it out, still as a tomb of granite. And all the time she is coming in her dark cloaks, moving through the catacombs beyond the mirror, and he knows she is bringing an infection called obsession. Sheets of dust are as shrouds in the winds of the labyrinths of death. In black leather and black helmets the motorcyclists are speeding towards his brain. The dark chevrolet is dawning on the house of Orphée.

Ripeness is all, for poets as for men. Pyres, pylons, worried forms, silence, an egg, water, ultimate chaos and a tribunal of birds known by the tribe to be elders. He types, and his eyes are becoming stones. Hands of rock, births and bones, the deeper stones, the birds, mountains, iron corridors beyond the page of the mirror, lipstick on glass. The end is inked in black and comes like a coda to his mind. There is no surprise in time. Lust is the condition of the homeward dust. There is a spiral as of lips and words, and a helix-wind of birds. She is here. With all her passion. Her hand stretches out to take his through the mirror infected with death. A candle is burning itself into a frenzy of shadows. Death is here. With her kiss. Her kiss.

Come, Orphée. The rest is silent, immutable and inexorable as the nature of the sea and its horizons. The chevrolet recedes with its henchmen in escort and the motors of hell are heard to be diminishing in audibility with all the pace of a cortège. The rest is an embrace. And indeed, silence.

(Based on the film Orphée, by Jean Cocteau)

and the angel spoke of snow

I remember the presence of the angel in the dust of the
silver dawn, amidst the fear & the broken glass when slivers
of the face of God shattered as the poor city woke to its
painful memories...

and I remember how the angel spoke of snow we could not
see for storms & how he shook the earth with his bright
emotion...

now I go among the white lakes of my mind, alive to the
birds as they sing of light & morning, while I walk on the
grass & the dew. and so I stand on the dusty land &
commend the dying to the sea, silent by a rose at dawn ...

dream

dreaming of God ...
this steel & stone of the moment,
carving of consciousness,
colourful show of dawn among willows –
an idea – white, sunlit, stunned,
a slight dew upon the grass, & way:
we are alive to the white leopard
of the falling of the light:
we think of Christ & Krishna
in the composition of a thought in waves –
& after a fine rain – the hum of spring –
this wild form or fabric
flowing with roses,
& the slow local flow
of sun & tongue,
becoming:

& it moves with a white infmity
we can touch like steel or stone,
as these moments of smoke
spiral from the land through deeper sky:
how we pace through light
in the stream of reality –
the escarpment of a dream,
layer upon layer
of light.:
in the latent mystery of the rising sun,
& the great sea of this world,
& in wave after wave of deep space,
we are dreaming
of a carving
of
the light